The **Military Spouse's Employment**

Pocket Guide

D1741371

Ron Krannich, Ph.D.

The Military Spouse's Employment Pocket Guide

Warning/Liability/Warranty: The author and publisher have made every attempt to provide the reader with accurate, timely, and useful information. However, given the rapid changes taking place in today's economy and job market, some information will inevitably change. The information presented here is for reference purposes only. The author and publisher make no claims that using this pocket guide will guarantee the reader a job. The author and/or publisher shall not be liable for any losses or damages incurred in the process of following the advice in this book.

ISBN: 978-1-57023-303-6 (13-digit); 1-57023-303-9 (10-digit)

Library of Congress: 2009923928

Publisher: For information on Impact Publications, including current and forthcoming publications, authors, press kits, online bookstore, newsletters, downloadable catalogs, and submission requirements, visit the left navigation bar on the front page of www.impactpublications.com.

Quantity Discounts: We offer quantity discounts on bulk purchases. Please review our discount schedule on page 60 and at www.impactpublications.com, or contact Special Sales Department: Tel. 703-361-0255.

Sales/Distribution: All sales and distribution inquiries should be directed to the publisher: Sales Department, IMPACT PUBLICATIONS, 9104-N Manassas Drive, Manassas Park, VA 20111-5211, Tel. 703-361-7300, Fax 703-335-9486, or email: query@impactpublications.com.

Author: Ron Krannich, Ph.D., is one of America's leading career and travel writers. Author of more than 80 books, he has written several bestsellers for military, students, and ex-offenders in transition. Many titles appearing in the order form (page 59) are authored by Dr. Krannich.

Contents

The Military Spouse's Employment World

Job Search Information and Skills

Job Survival and Success

Documentation/Contacts

Military Spouse Employment Assistance

During the past 25 years the military has increasingly recognized the importance of helping military spouses find **jobs** and develop **portable careers** (page 8) that are compatible with the military's lifestyle and retention goals. Today initiatives center around the Family Employment Readiness Programs (FERP) attached to family support centers of various services:

- Army . . . . Army Community Service Centers
- Navy . . . . Fleet and Family Support Centers
- Air Force . . . . Airman and Family Readiness Centers
- Marine Corps . . . . Family Services Centers
- Coast Guard . . . . Work Life Programs

In addition, military transition assistance centers on all bases offer spousal employment assistance for transitioning families as part of their Transition Assistance Program (TAP).

One of the first things you should do upon arriving in a new location is contact your appropriate family services office about military spouse employment opportunities and related support services. Most of these offices offer the following assistance:

- individual testing, counseling, and support
- job search skills training (writing resumes, interviewing)
- critiquing resumes, applications, and job search letters
- networking opportunities
- job listings with and referrals to local employers
- access to computers and the Internet
- information on federal jobs and applications
- use of copy machines, faxes, and telephones
- referrals to local job clubs and placement firms
- access to employment resources (books, magazines, DVDs)

- information on Military Spouse Preference (MSP) program for DoD jobs and Career Advancement Accounts (CAA) for spouses (pays up to $3,000 a year for education and training at some locales)
- Family Readiness Groups

Personnel staffing these family service centers provide assistance and support – invaluable for anyone embarking on a job search that is often filled with anxiety, rejections, and disappointments when done alone. Get to know your Center's personnel and services – they may become your best resource!

My Local Family Service Center

Name _____

Address _____

_____

Tel. _____

Website: _____

Email: _____

Key contacts (names): _____

_____

Services I plan to use through the Center:

1. _____   3. _____

2. _____   4. _____

You also should acquire a copy of our companion pocket guide to military bases and services – *The Military Spouse's Map Through the Maze Pocket Guide* (see pages 59-60).

Recognize Your Barriers to Employment

Most people face several barriers to employment. As a military spouse you need to recognize **your barriers** and take appropriate actions to overcome those you can change or eliminate. While some barriers may be **external** (beyond your control), others are **internal** (within your control). **External barriers**, for example, might include the following:

- **Institutional:** Military/base rules, practices, and protocols – frequent relocations, disruptive deployments, child care, employment restrictions. State residence, licensing, and certification requirements.

- **Situational**: Your location, family, weather/climate, spouse's job.

- **Personal:** Your age, height, disabilities, current number of children.

Examples of your **internal barriers** – those things within your control to change – include:

- **Personal:** Your weight, attitude, personality, self-esteem, addictions, habits, assertiveness, networks, planning, time management, financial management, volunteering, housing, transportation, marital relationship, parenting responsibilities and skills, and child care costs.

- **Professional:** Your education, training, workplace skills, work experience, job search skills, communication skills, computer skills, Internet access, licenses, and certifications.

The key to employment success is knowing what you can and cannot change and focus on changing those things that are within your **power to change**. It may, for example, mean making decisions that result in taking the following actions:

- losing weight
- lowering stress and anxiety
- eating nutritiously
- exercising more
- managing addictive behaviors (tobacco, alcohol, drugs)
- improving self-esteem
- becoming more assertive
- strengthening mental wellness
- acquiring more education and training
- meeting state licensing and certification requirements
- planning daily and weekly schedules
- budgeting personal finances
- changing spending habits
- managing time
- developing effective job search skills
- arranging child care
- organizing transportation

Overcome Barriers to Employment Plan

Complete the following exercises relating to your barriers:

My top five employment barriers

1. _____ I S P

2. _____ I S P

3. _____ I S P

4. _____ I S P

5. _____ I S P

Review your list on page 4 and indicate whether or not each one is an Institutional (**I**), Situational (**S**), or Personal (**P**) employment barrier by circling the appropriate letter at the end of each barrier statement.

Now, list what five actions you will take within the next two months to eliminate employment barriers that are **within your power to change**:

Five actions I will take in the next 60 days to eliminate my employment barriers:

1. _____

_____

2. _____

_____

3. _____

_____

4. _____

_____

5. _____

_____

How's Your Attitude?

Your attitude may well become your most important **asset** in both work and life – or it may get in your way. Indeed, we consider it to be the first key step in conducting an effective job search (see page 31). Take a moment to examine your attitude. Does your attitude show in what you say and do? Are others attracted to you in a positive manner? Do you have a "can do" attitude that propels you to success or a "can't do" attitude that drags you down? Do you start the morning by looking forward to having a wonderful day or do you dread getting up? Do you make excuses and complain a lot or do you take responsibility for your actions? Are you a positive or negative person who tends to attract negativity in your life?

Check the current state of your attitude by completing the following exercise. Indicate whether or not you primarily **agree** ("Yes") or **disagree** ("No") with each statement:

		Yes	No
1.	Other people often make my work and life difficult.	❏	❏
2.	When I get into trouble, it's often because of what someone else did rather than my fault.	❏	❏
3.	People often take advantage of me.	❏	❏
4.	When I worked, people less qualified than me often got promoted.	❏	❏
5.	I avoid taking risks because I'm afraid of failing.	❏	❏
6.	I don't trust many people.	❏	❏
7.	Not many people trust me.	❏	❏
8.	Not many people I know take responsibility.	❏	❏
9.	Most people get ahead because of connections, schmoozing, and politics.	❏	❏
10.	When I worked, I was assigned more duties than other people in similar positions.	❏	❏

11. I expect to be discriminated against in my job search and on the job. ❏ ❏
12. I don't feel like I can change many things; I've been dealt this hand, so I'll have to live with it. ❏ ❏
13. I've had my share of bad luck. ❏ ❏
14. Employers try to take advantage of job seekers by offering them low salaries. ❏ ❏
15. I didn't like many of the people I worked with. ❏ ❏
16. There's not much I can do to get ahead. ❏ ❏
17. My ideas are not really taken seriously. ❏ ❏
18. I often think of reasons why other people's ideas won't work. ❏ ❏
19. Other people are often wrong, but I have to put up with them nonetheless. ❏ ❏
20. I sometimes respond to suggestions by saying "Yes, but . . . ," "I'm not sure . . . ," "I don't think it will work . . . ," "Let's not do that . . ." ❏ ❏
21. I don't see why I need to get more education. ❏ ❏
22. I often wish other people would just disappear. ❏ ❏
23. I sometimes feel depressed. ❏ ❏
24. I have a hard time getting and staying motivated. ❏ ❏
25. I don't look forward to going to work. ❏ ❏
26. When I worked, I sometimes came to work late. ❏ ❏
27. The jobs I've had didn't reflect my true talents. ❏ ❏
28. I'm worth more than most employers will pay. ❏ ❏
29. I've been known to do things behind my boss's back that could get me into trouble. ❏ ❏

TOTALS __ __

If you checked "Yes" to more than six of these statements, you may be harboring some negative attitudes that affect both your job search and your on-the-job performance. You should seriously consider changing these attitudes since they are most likely significant **barriers to getting ahead** in work and life!

Military Spouse-Friendly Jobs

Military spouses tend to work in numerous occupations related to many of these base employers and flexible/portable careers:

Popular Jobs/Careers for Military Spouses

1. Commissary/exchange worker
2. Consultant/financial planner
3. Administration/office worker
4. Teacher and childcare worker
5. Nurse/health care worker
6. Government worker
7. Real estate agent
8. Customer service rep
9. Telemarketer
10. Contract/temporary worker

DoD has identified these **five high-growth portable career fields** as being suitable to the mobile military lifestyle:

- **Health care:** Nursing, health technology (radiology, x-ray, chemo), pharmacology, dental hygiene, medical record management, etc.
- **Financial services:** Banking, mortgages, insurance, investment, real estate, financial counseling, etc.
- **Information technology:** computer networking, systems, administration, web development, software design, help desk
- **Education:** Teacher, teacher's aide, curriculum, administration
- **Construction trades:** Electrician, plumber, carpenter, brick mason

What three jobs appeal to you – ones you would do well and enjoy doing? (Visit http://online.onetcenter.org and www.bls.gov/oco for dozens of job and career ideas):

1. _____
2. _____
3. _____

Community-Based Opportunity Networks

A **community** is more than just a place to live, work, and raise a family. It consists of many interacting and mutually dependent **players** – individuals, groups, organizations, and institutions – that cooperate and compete with one another. You can easily identify these players in the Yellow Pages of your local telephone book. Examples of such players include:

- Banks/financial organizations
- Schools/training groups
- Colleges and universities
- Retail/wholesale businesses
- Direct sales businesses
- Churches/temples/synagogues
- Nonprofit organizations
- Volunteer organizations
- Federal government agencies
- State government agencies
- Local government agencies
- Military bases/associations
- Professional associations
- Clubs/community groups
- Media groups
- Law firms/lawyers
- Law enforcement/security
- Hospitals/clinics
- Public health groups
- Doctors/health professionals
- Transportation firms
- Construction firms
- Temporary employment firms
- One-Stop Career Centers
- Staffing/placement firms
- Auto dealers/suppliers
- Real estate/property firms
- Shippers (UPS, FedEx)
- Communication firms
- Courts/judicial centers
- Substance abuse centers
- Mental health/wellness groups
- Contractors/consultants
- Restaurants/food outlets

These players should be viewed as **opportunity structures** for finding jobs through informal, word-of-mouth channels. They become important **networks** for locating job opportunities. The following figure illustrates the dynamic **structure** of communities and how the key players **interrelate**:

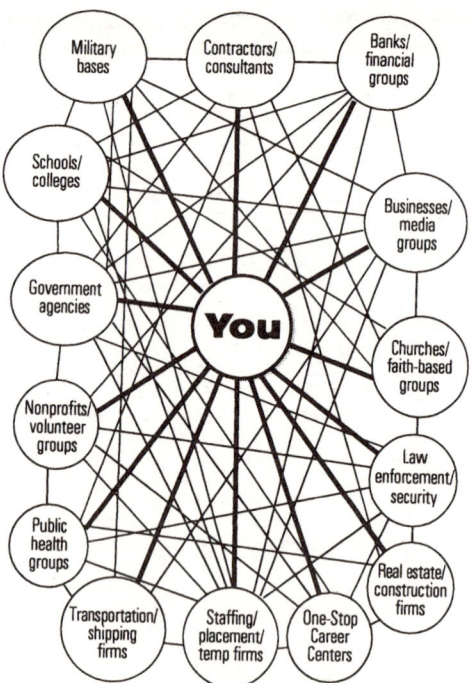

Take a yellow highlighter and identify those community players (color the circles) you plan to contact and interact with during the next month as you conduct a community-based job search.

Military Spouse-Friendly Employers

Many employers are very receptive to hiring military spouses as well as transitioning military personnel. For starters, check out the annual (June) survey results published by the *Military Spouse Magazine* (www.milspouse.com), which reveals the top 10 employers that hire military spouses. For the year 2008, the following employers/companies were identified as the most receptive for hiring military spouses:

Top 10 Military Spouse-Friendly Employers, 2008

1.	Health Net, Inc.	www.healthnet.com
2.	USAA	www.usaa.com
3.	Sunbelt Rentals, Inc.	www.sunbeltrentals.com
4.	West Corporation	www.west.com
5.	RE/MAX	www.remax.com
6.	Wachovia Corporation	www.wachovia.com
7.	Kelly Services, Inc.	www.kellyservices.com
8.	Manpower Inc.	www.manpower.com
9.	The Home Depot, Inc.	www.homedepot.com
10.	Computer Services Corp.	www.csc.com

Since these are nationwide employers/companies, they may or may not have a presence in your community. Therefore, it's important that you identify military spouse-friendly employers located in your particular community (see page 13).

Also, review the annual (March) survey conducted by *G.I. Jobs* (www.gijobs.com) on the top 50 military-friendly employers:

1. Johnson Controls — www.johnsoncontrols.com
2. BNSF Railway — www.bnsf.com/careers/military
3. Union Pacific — www.unionpacific.jobs
4. USAA — www.usaa.apply2jobs.com
5. ITT Corporation — www.itt.com/careers
6. Mantech International — www.mantech.com/careers
7. Applied Materials — www.appliedmaterials.com/careers
8. CSX Transportation — www.csx.com/?fuseaction=careers. keepintouch
9. The Home Depot — http://careers.homedepot.com/military
10. EG&G — www.urscorp.com/careers
11. CINTAS Corporation — www.cintas.com/careers/career paths/junior_military_ncos.aspx
12. Lockheed Martin — www.lockheedmartinjobs.com
13. Schneider National, Inc. — www.schneiderjobs.com
14. J.B. Hunt Transport, Inc. — www.jbhunt.com/jobs
15. Fluor Corporation — www.fluor.com/military
16. General Electric — www.ge.com/careers/veterans
17. Booz Allen Hamilton — www.boozallen.com/careers
18. Brinks U.S. — www.us.brinksinc.com/careers
19. DynCorp International — www.dyncorprecruiting.com
20. Transocean, Inc. — www.deepwater.com/usjobs
21. Freeport-McMoRan — www.fcx.com/careers/current.htm
22. Sunbelt Rentals, Inc. — www.sunbeltrentals.com/about/ careers.aspx
23. Werner Enterprises — www.werner.com/content/careers/ jobs/home
24. Southern Company — www.southerncompany.com/career info/military.aspx
25. Sears Holdings — www.searsholdings.com/careers/military
26. Progress Energy — www.progress-energy.com/aboutus/ employment
27. American Electric Power — www.aep.com/careers
28. Sprint Nextel — http://about.sprint.com/careers
29. State Farm Insurance Co. — www.statefarm.com/careers
30. Norfolk Southern — www.nscorp.com/careers

31.	Travelers	www.travelers.com/careers
32.	Northrop Grumman Corp.	http://careers.northropgrumman.com
33.	Health Net, Inc.	www.careersathealthnet.com
34.	BearingPoint, Inc.	www.bearingpoint.jobs
35.	Merrill Lynch	(closed 2009)
36.	CACI	www.caci.com/jobs/vets
37.	The Boeing Company	www.boeing.com/employment
38.	Bank of America	http://careers.bankofamerica.com/military
39.	Sodexo	www.sodexohireseroes.com
40.	AAR	http://employment.aarcorp.com
41.	Lowe's Companies, Inc.	http://careers.lowes.com
42.	Exelon	www.exeloncorp.com/careers
43.	Chrysler LLC	www.chryslerllc.com/en/community/military support
44.	G4S Wackenhut	http://www.g4s.com/usw
45.	Ecolab Lnc.	www.ecolab.com/careers
46.	Ensco International	www.enscointernational.com
47.	Corrections Corporation of America	www.correctionscorp.com/careers
48.	Southern California Edison	www.edison.com/careers
49.	Harris Corporation	www.harris.com/harris/careers
50.	T-Mobile	www.t-mobile.com/jobs

Which of the above spouse- and military-friendly companies have operations and job opportunities in your community?

_____

_____

_____

_____

_____

_____

_____

_____

_____

Research and Contact Local Employers

Identify the top three employers in your community by category:

Employers on base (may give military spouse preference)

1. _____
2. _____
3. _____

Government offices/agencies (federal, state, and/or local)

1. _____
2. _____
3. _____

Nonprofit organizations (hospitals, charities, churches, clubs)

1. _____
2. _____
3. _____

Educational institutions/groups (schools, colleges, universities, testing centers, tutoring groups, day-care centers, associations)

1. _____
2. _____
3. _____

Businesses (full-time hourly/salaried, from small to large companies)

1. _____
2. _____
3. _____

Businesses (part-time hourly/salaried, from small to large companies)

1. _____
2. _____
3. _____

Businesses (commission-driven sales/flexible work schedules)

1. _____
2. _____
3. _____

Self-employment (direct-sales, virtual assistant, consulting)

1. _____
2. _____
3. _____

I plan to research and contact the following employers during the next two weeks:

1. _____
2. _____
3. _____

Finding a Federal Job

Many spouses find rewarding jobs and portable careers with the federal government. In fact, today it's much easier for military spouses to land a federal job since they are now (September 2008 – Executive Order 13463, 73 FR 56703) exempted from the competitive service for certain positions.

If you are interested in landing a federal job, do the following:

1. **Visit your family services center** for information on federal agencies in your community, the application process, and hiring preferences and exempted positions for military spouses.

2. **Survey job vacancies** online at www.usajobs.gov and follow the specified application process.

3. **Read the vacancy announcement carefully**, determine your eligibility, and then carefully follow the application instructions.

4. **Submit an outstanding application** (OF612 or resume) by following the seasoned advice and examples found in these three key books on federal employment (see page 59 or www.impactpublications.com):

   - *The Book of U.S. Government Jobs* ($22.95)
   - *Federal Resume Guidebook* ($21.95)
   - *Ten Steps to a Federal Job, With CD-ROM* ($28.95)

Key Websites for Assistance and Support

Military Spouse Job/Placement Websites
- Military Spouse Career Center   www.military.com/spouse
- Military Spouse Corporate
  Career Network (MSCCN)   www.msccn.org

Virtual Jobs for Military Spouses Websites
- Staffcentrix   www.staffcentrix.com
- VSS CyberOffice   www.vsscyberoffice.com

Military Spouse/Family-Friendly Websites
- Army Wife Talk Radio   www.armywifetalkradio.com
- CareerOneStop (military spouses)   www.careeronestop.org/military transition/militarySpouses.aspx
- CincHouse   www.cinchouse.com
- DefenseLink   www.defenselink.mil
- Help! I'm a Military Spouse   www.militaryspousehelp.com
- Jenny the Military Spouse   www.jennyspouse.com
- Military Home Front   www.militaryhomefront.dod.mil
- Military Money Magazine   www.militarymoney.com
- Military Officers Association
  of America (MOAA)   www.moaa.org
- Military OneSource   www.militaryonesource.com
- Military Spouse Coach   www.militaryspousecoach.com
- Military Spouse Magazine   www.milspouse.com
- Military Spouse Resource Center   www.MilSpouse.org
- Military Spouse Support Network   www.militaryspousesupport.net
- Military Wives   www.militarywives.com
- National Military Family Assoc.   www.nmfa.org
- Non-Commissioned Officers
  Association (NCOA)   www.ncoausa.org
- Servicemembers Opportunity
  Colleges (SOC)   www.soc.aascu.org
- SGT Mom's   www.sgtmoms.com

Official Military Family Websites

- Army   www.armywell-being.org
- Air Force   www.afcrossroads.com
- Navy & Marine Corps   www.lifelines.navy.mil
- Coast Guard   www.uscg.mil
- Army & Air National Guards   www.guardfamily.org

Other useful websites I've discovered!

_____

_____

_____

Useful Books for Military Spouses
(order through page 58 and www.impactpublications.com)

- *The 2-Second Commute*
- *Armed Forces Guide to Personal Financial Planning*
- *Chicken Soup for the Military Wife's Soul*
- *The Complete Idiot's Guide to Life as a Military Spouse*
- *A Family's Guide to the Military for Dummies*
- *Help! I'm a Military Spouse – I Get a Life Too!*
- *Heroes At Home*
- *Homefront Club*
- *In Harm's Way*
- *Jobs and the Military Spouse*
- *Married to the Military*
- *The Military Spouse's Complete Guide to Career Success*
- *Navy Spouse's Guide*
- *New Relocating Spouse's Guide to Employment*
- *Surviving Deployment*
- *Today's Military Wife*
- *Virtual Assistant*
- *Your Military Family Network*

Education Snapshot

Highest formal education level attained:

☐ 8ᵗʰ grade
☐ high school diploma or GED
☐ some college (years completed: _____)
☐ associate degree (specify: _____)
☐ four-year college degree (specify:_____)
☐ graduate degree (specify: _____)
☐ other (specify: _____)

Schools attended beyond 8ᵗʰ grade, with dates:

Name	Location	Dates

Special licenses/certificates, with dates:

_____

_____

_____

_____

Education/Training Details

High school attended:

Name _____

Address _____

_____

Years attended: _____ to _____

Highest grade completed: 9   10   11   12

Diploma: ❑ Yes ❑ No   GPA (4.0 system): _____

Other high schools attended (names/dates):

_____

_____

High school equivalent:

❑ GED (year: _____)   ❑ Other (_____)

Favorite subjects:

_____

Major accomplishments:

_____

_____

Most Recent College/University Attended:

Name _____

Address _____

_____

Accredited institution: ❑ Yes ❑ No

Type: ❑ residential   ❑ distance learning/online

Years attended: _____ to _____

Credit hours completed: _____ GPA: _____

Major(s): _____

Minor(s): _____

Degree: ❑ Yes   ❑ No (When expect? _____)

Key skills acquired: _____

_____

_____

Key accomplishments: _____

_____

_____

_____

Other College/University Attended:

Name _____

Address _____

_____

Accredited institution: ❑ Yes ❑ No

Type: ❑ residential   ❑ distance learning/online

Years attended: _____ to _____

Credit hours completed: _____ GPA: _____

Major(s): _____

Minor(s): _____

Degree: ❑ Yes ❑ No

Key skills acquired: _____

_____

_____

Key accomplishments:_____

_____

_____

_____

_____

Other Education/Training Experience:

Name _____

Location _____

_____

Length of program (specify one):

   Days (__) Weeks (__) Months (__) Years (__)

Dates: From _____ to _____

Type of experience: _____

_____

_____

Certificate, degree, diploma received: _____

_____

Key skills acquired: _____

_____

_____

Equipment or tools used in training: _____

_____

_____

Other Education/Training Experience:

Name _____

Location _____

_____

Length of program (specify one):

    Days (__) Weeks (__) Months (__) Years (__)

Dates: From _____ to _____

Type of experience: _____

_____

_____

Certificate, degree, diploma received: _____

_____

Key skills acquired: _____

_____

_____

Equipment or tools used in training: _____

_____

_____

Work History/Experience – Job #1

Employer _____

Street address _____

City, state, ZIP code _____

Website _____

Phone number _____

Job title _____

Employment dates: From _____ to _____

Salary: Start _____   End _____

Raises: ☐ Yes   ☐ No   Promotions: ☐ Yes   ☐ No

Job duties and responsibilities: _____

_____

Major skills used: _____

_____

Major accomplishments: _____

_____

_____

Reason for leaving: _____

Supervisor's name: _____

Work History/Experience – Job #2

Employer _____

Street address _____

City, state, ZIP code _____

Website _____

Phone number _____

Job title _____

Employment dates: From _____ To _____

Salary: Start _____ End _____

Raises: ☐ Yes ☐ No   Promotions: ☐ Yes ☐ No

Job duties and responsibilities: _____

_____

Major skills used: _____

_____

Major accomplishments: _____

_____

_____

Reason for leaving: _____

Supervisor's name: _____

Work History/Experience – Job #3

Employer _____

Street address _____

City, state, ZIP code _____

Website _____

Phone number _____

Job title _____

Employment dates: From _____ To _____

Salary: Start _____ End _____

Raises: ☐ Yes ☐ No   Promotions: ☐ Yes ☐ No

Job duties and responsibilities: _____

_____

Major skills used: _____

_____

Major accomplishments: _____

_____

_____

Reason for leaving: _____

Supervisor's name: _____

Other Noteworthy Experiences

Identify any experiences that might strengthen your resume, applications, and interviews – ones indicating important transferable skills, work behaviors, and personality characteristics.

Professional memberships and associations: _____

_____

Honors and awards: _____

_____

Volunteer/community work: _____

_____

Hobbies and interests: _____

_____

Leadership roles: _____

_____

Family responsibilities: _____

_____

Other: _____

_____

Identify Your Best References

Contact your references **before** including them on your list.
Tell them about your job search, ask if they would be willing to
give you a **positive reference**, and send them your resume.
Employers are most impressed with **work references**.

Work/Professional Reference #1:

Name _____

Title _____

Street address _____

City, state, ZIP code _____

Phone: _____ Email: _____

Relationship to you: _____

Work/Professional Reference #2:

Name _____

Title _____

Company _____

Street address _____

City, state, ZIP code _____

Phone: _____ Email: _____

Relationship to you: _____

Work/Professional Reference #3:

Name _____

Title _____

Company _____

Street address _____

City, state, ZIP code _____

Phone: _____ Email: _____

Relationship to you: _____

Personal Reference #1:

Name _____

Street address _____

City, state, ZIP code _____

Phone: _____ Email: _____

Relationship to you: _____

Personal Reference #2:

Name _____

Street address _____

City, state, ZIP code _____

Phone: _____ Email: _____

Relationship to you: _____

10 Steps to Job Search Success

Finding a job involves a 10-step process. Each step includes specific job search activities that should be conducted in sequence. Unfortunately, many job seekers start with Step 7 – complete applications and write resumes – without going through the previous six steps that are critical for producing powerful applications and resumes. Smart and effective job seekers follow these 10 job search steps in this order:

1. Get motivated with winning attitudes

2. Seek assistance and become proactive

3. Select appropriate job search approaches

4. Assess your skills and identify your motivated abilities and skills (MAS)

5. Develop a powerful objective

6. Conduct research on jobs, employers, and communities

7. Write effective applications, resumes, and letters

8. Network for information, advice, and referrals

9. Develop winning job interview skills

10. Negotiate salary and benefits like a pro

Identify Your Transferable Skills

You have dozens of transferable skills that can be used in different work settings. Check the ones you possess:

Organizational and Interpersonal Skills

- ❑ communicating
- ❑ problem solving
- ❑ analyzing
- ❑ planning
- ❑ decision-making
- ❑ trouble-shooting
- ❑ implementing
- ❑ understanding
- ❑ setting goals
- ❑ innovating
- ❑ thinking logically
- ❑ evaluating
- ❑ synthesizing
- ❑ forecasting

- ❑ motivating
- ❑ leading
- ❑ selling
- ❑ performing
- ❑ reviewing
- ❑ team building
- ❑ coaching
- ❑ supervising
- ❑ negotiating
- ❑ administering
- ❑ conceptualizing
- ❑ generalizing
- ❑ managing time
- ❑ creating

- ❑ judging
- ❑ controlling
- ❑ organizing
- ❑ persuading
- ❑ improving
- ❑ designing
- ❑ consulting
- ❑ teaching/training
- ❑ advising
- ❑ interpreting
- ❑ achieving
- ❑ reporting
- ❑ managing
- ❑ multi-tasking

Personality and Work-Style Traits

- ❑ diligent
- ❑ patient
- ❑ dependable
- ❑ persistent
- ❑ tactful
- ❑ loyal
- ❑ successful
- ❑ versatile
- ❑ enthusiastic
- ❑ outgoing
- ❑ expressive
- ❑ adaptable
- ❑ democratic
- ❑ resourceful
- ❑ creative

- ❑ objective
- ❑ warm
- ❑ honest
- ❑ reliable
- ❑ perceptive
- ❑ assertive
- ❑ sensitive
- ❑ astute
- ❑ easygoing
- ❑ flexible
- ❑ competent
- ❑ punctual
- ❑ receptive
- ❑ diplomatic
- ❑ self-confident

- ❑ tenacious
- ❑ discreet
- ❑ talented
- ❑ empathic
- ❑ orderly
- ❑ tolerant
- ❑ frank
- ❑ cooperative
- ❑ self-starter
- ❑ effective
- ❑ tidy
- ❑ candid
- ❑ firm
- ❑ sincere
- ❑ efficient

Motivated Abilities & Skills (MAS)

The single most important piece of information you need about yourself is your Motivated Abilities and Skills (MAS) – your **recurring patterns of accomplishments**. You identify these by analyzing your **past achievements** – those things you do well, enjoy doing, and want to continue doing in the future. You should organize your job search around your MAS in order to find jobs that best **fit** your pattern. I detail the process for identifying your MAS in *I Want to Do Something Else, But I'm Not Sure What It Is* (Impact Publications, see page 59).

Start identifying your Motivated Abilities and Skills (MAS) by responding to these two questions:

1. **What abilities and skills have I always enjoyed using and want to continue using in the future?**

    _____

    _____

2. **What jobs are the best fit for my MAS?** (**TIP:** Review the 1,000+ jobs in the *The O*NET Dictionary of Occupational Titles*, which is found in libraries or online: http://online.onetcenter.org. Also, survey the 285+ occupations at www.bls.gov/OCO.)

    _____

    _____

State a Clear Objective or Goal

Stating a clear career objective or goal will help you target your job search and communicate your major **strengths** (skills and abilities) to employers. Best of all, it will clarify what it is you **want to do** as well as what you **can do** for the employer. Without a clear goal, you may appear disorganized and unfocused – you can do *"a little of this, a little of that"* but nothing in particular to convince employers that you can do **their job**.

Stating a powerful career goal or objective in under 25 words is one of the toughest job search tasks. It may take hours or days to formulate one that best reflects your key motivations, abilities, and skills – your MAS. Nonetheless, you **must** do this if you want to give your job search a **clear direction**.

Try to formulate an objective or goal that follows this simple but powerful **skill-outcome formula** focused on the **needs of employers**:

I would like a job where I can use my ability to

_____, *which will result in*

_____ *for an employer.*

Here's an example of a **weak objective** that also is very **self-centered** rather than employer-centered:

A Landscape Design position with opportunity for advancement

© Impact Publications – copying strictly prohibited

Here's an example of a much **stronger objective** that also is very **employer-centered**:

> To use innovative **landscape design** training for developing award-winning approaches to designing commercial properties.

Now formulate your own 25- to 30-word career or job objective using the same skill-outcome formula which focuses on the needs of employers:

_____

_____

_____

_____

_____

Once you have refined your objective, be sure to communicate it on your resume and applications as well as in cover letters and other types of correspondence with employers.

For more information on how to develop a powerful career objective, see the following book (available on page 59):

I Want to Do Something Else But I'm Not Sure What It Is: Find a Job That's Fit for You (Impact Publications, 2005, pp. 116-140)

Complete Winning Applications

Most employers require employment applications – paper or electronic. These are key **screening devices** that should represent your **best effort** to get your foot in the employer's door. Treat them as you would a first date – make a great first impression! For more information, see *Resume, Application, and Letter Tips for People With Hot and Not-So-Hot Backgrounds* (Impact Publications, 2006). The following tips will help you produce first-rate applications for getting interviews:

1. Complete each section thoroughly. If something does not relate to you, write "N/A" (not applicable)
2. Answer all questions completely – take time to do it right.
3. Dress nicely for the application site – may get interviewed.
4. Read the instructions carefully and follow completely.
5. Use an erasable black pen to make clean changes.
6. Write as neatly as possible – it reflects on your style.
7. Include all previous employers – no obvious time gaps.
8. If you lack work experience, be creative in revealing your key abilities and transferable skills.
9. Appear educated, even if you lack formal credentials.
10. Select your references carefully – only positive ones.
11. Handle red flag questions honestly and tactfully – reference "see me" or "will discuss at the interview."
12. Minimize abbreviations and jargon.
13. Avoid vague statements – employers want details.
14. Avoid revealing salary information if possible.
15. Emphasize your motivated abilities and skills throughout.
16. Remember to sign and date the application.
17. Re-read your answers – be complete and error-free.
18. Attach an achievement-oriented resume if appropriate.
19. Ask about the selection process and hiring decision.
20. Follow up your application with a telephone call.

Avoid Common Resume Mistakes

Resumes are important advertisements for interviews. However, few people are resume savvy – most produce "dead upon arrival" resumes. They make numerous writing, production, and distribution mistakes. Avoid these 25 **writing errors**:

1. Unrelated to the position in question.
2. Too long or too short.
3. Unattractive – poorly designed, small type style, crowded copy.
4. Misspellings, poor grammar, wordiness, and repetition.
5. Punctuation errors.
6. Lengthy phrases, long sentences, and awkward paragraphs.
7. Slick, amateurish, or "gimmicky" – appears over-produced.
8. Boastful, egocentric, and aggressive.
9. Dishonest, untrustworthy, or suspicious information.
10. Missing critical categories – experience, skills, and education.
11. Difficult to interpret because of poor organization and lack of focus.
12. Unexplained time gaps between jobs.
13. Too many jobs – job hopper with no career advancement.
14. No evidence of past accomplishments or a pattern of performance.
15. Lacks credibility and content – includes "canned" resume language.
16. States a strange, unclear, or vague objective.
17. Appears over-qualified or under-qualified for the position.
18. Includes personal information that does not enhance the resume.
19. Lacks critical contact information (telephone number and email).
20. Uses jargon and abbreviations unfamiliar to the reader.
21. Embellishes name with formal titles, middle names, and nicknames.
22. Repeatedly refers to "I" and appears self-centered.
23. Includes self-serving references that raise credibility questions.
24. Includes red flag information such as being incarcerated or fired.
25. Sloppy, with handwritten corrections and/or stains or smudges.

Employers also report encountering several of these 20 **production, distribution, and follow-up errors**:

1. Poorly typed and reproduced – hard to read.
2. Produced on odd-sized paper.
3. Printed on poor quality paper or on extremely thin or thick paper.
4. Soiled with stains, fingerprints, or ink marks.
5. Sent to the wrong person or department.
6. Mailed, faxed, or emailed to "To Whom It May Concern."
7. Emailed as an attachment which could have a virus if opened.
8. Enclosed in a tiny envelope that requires the resume to be unfolded and flattened several times.
9. Arrived without proper postage – the employer gets to pay the extra!
10. Sent the resume by the slowest postage rate possible.
11. Envelope double-sealed with tape and nearly indestructible!
12. Back of envelope includes a handwritten note stating that something is missing – a telephone number, email, or new mailing address.
13. Resume taped to the inside of the envelope.
14. Accompanied by inappropriate enclosures – self-serving letters or recommendations, transcripts, or work samples.
15. Arrived too late for consideration.
16. Came without a cover letter.
17. Cover letter repeated what was on the resume.
18. Sent the same resume to the same person several times.
19. Follow-up call made too soon – before the resume and letter arrived!
20. Follow-up call was too aggressive – candidate appeared needy.

Your resume, instead, should incorporate these five characteristics of **strong and effective resumes**:

1. Clearly communicate your purpose and competencies in relation to employers' needs.
2. Be concise and easy to read.
3. Outline a pattern of success highlighted with accomplishments.
4. Motivate the reader to read it in-depth.
5. Tell employers that you are a responsible and purposeful individual – a doer who can solve their problems.

For seasoned resume advice and great examples, see *High Impact Resumes and Letters* (Impact Publications), page 59.

Use the Internet Wisely

Contrary to what many people believe, few job seekers actually find jobs online – maybe 20 percent. But job seekers tend to spend a disproportionate amount of time looking for jobs on such mega websites as www.monster.com, www.careerbuilder.com, and http://hotjobs.yahoo.com. Indeed, the Internet can be a tremendous time waster – gives **false hopes** to job seekers who actually believe their next job will be found on the Internet! Disappointed, many resign themselves to the mistaken beliefs that *"There are no jobs out there for me. No one will hire me!"*

Smart job seekers, which should include you, understand how to best use the Internet in their job search. They do the following:

1. Post their resume to several employment websites – both general and specialty sites. They tend to have better luck with specialty sites. Military spouses visit www.militarycom/spouse and www.msccn.org.
2. Respond to job listings that best fit their interests, skills, and abilities.
3. Spend most of their Internet time doing research on employers and jobs and responding to online application systems of companies.
4. Regularly use email to network and communicate with employers – from job inquiries to sending resumes and thank-you notes.
5. Move on to more productive job search activities, such as making cold calls, using voicemail, and networking face-to-face – activities not involving the Internet beyond regularly communicating by email.

As part of your job search arsenal, you need access to these two items:

- A computer with Internet access.
- An email address.

If you don't have these two basic items, you should do the following:

1. Use someone else's computer – from friend, relative, family services center, public library, or public employment office (One-Stop Center)
2. Get an email address. Use these free email services: www.gmail.google.com, www.mail.yahoo.com, and www.hotmail.com.

Network Your Way to Success

Most people look for jobs by submitting applications or resumes in response to job vacancies. However, the best way to find a job is to network with family, friends, and acquaintances – asking them for job information, advice, and referrals. Test your networking I.Q. with this exercise:

INSTRUCTIONS: Respond to each statement by circling the number to the right that best represents your situation. The higher your score, the higher your "Savvy Networking IQ."

SCALE:
5 = Strongly agree   2 = Disagree
4 = Agree   1 = Strongly disagree
3 = Maybe, not certain

1. I enjoy going to business and social functions where I have an opportunity to meet people.	5 4 3 2 1
2. I usually take the initiative in introducing myself to people I don't know.	5 4 3 2 1
3. I have a friendly and engaging personality that attracts others to me.	5 4 3 2 1
4. I seldom have a problem starting a conversation and engaging in small talk with strangers.	5 4 3 2 1
5. I usually return phone calls in a timely manner.	5 4 3 2 1
6. If I can't get through to someone on the phone, I'll keep trying until I do, even if it means making 10 more calls.	5 4 3 2 1
7. I have friends who will give me job leads.	5 4 3 2 1
8. I know at least 25 people who can give me career advice and referrals.	5 4 3 2 1
9. I don't mind approaching people with my professional concerns.	5 4 3 2 1

10. I'm good at asking questions and getting useful advice from others. 5 4 3 2 1

11. I usually handle rejections in stride by learning from them and moving on. 5 4 3 2 1

12. I make it a habit to stay in touch with members of my network by telephone, email, and letter. 5 4 3 2 1

13. I have a great network of individuals whom I can call on at anytime for assistance, and they will be happy to help me. 5 4 3 2 1

14. I belong to several organizations, including a professional association. 5 4 3 2 1

15. I consider myself an effective networker who never abuses my relationships. 5 4 3 2 1

TOTAL SCORE (I.Q.) [ ]

If your total composite I.Q. is above 65, you're most likely a savvy networker. If you're below 45, you're probably lacking key networking skills. You need to strengthen them.

Who is in your network? Develop a list of people whom you might contact for job information, advice, referrals, and leads. They should include the following:

- ❏ Friends (see Christmas list)
- ❏ Relatives (close/distant)
- ❏ Neighbors (present/former)
- ❏ Social acquaintances
- ❏ Classmates
- ❏ College alumni
- ❏ Teachers
- ❏ Bank managers
- ❏ Co-workers
- ❏ Online linkages/social networks
- ❏ Ministers/church members
- ❏ Association contacts
- ❏ Club members
- ❏ Direct-sales people
- ❏ Your doctor/dentist/optician
- ❏ Your lawyer/accountant
- ❏ Your insurance agent
- ❏ Tradespeople
- ❏ Former employers
- ❏ Fellow workers

Prepare for Job Interviews

The interview is the most important step to getting a job offer. It's also the most stressful job search activity. Here are some useful tips for preparing for a job interview:

1. Develop a 30-second pitch on why someone should hire you.
2. Review your resume and be prepared to discuss everything that appears on it – no ifs, ands, or buts.
3. Practice developing positive answers to frequently asked interview questions – stand in front of a mirror and record your answers.
4. Prepare positive answers to any objections to your background, experience, and skills.
5. Identify at least 10 questions you want to ask the interviewer.
6. Select a suitable interview wardrobe – neat, clean, and appropriate for the employer and company.
7. Confirm the time and place of the interview and arrive at the site five to 10 minutes early.
8. Treat everyone you meet, including receptionists, with enthusiasm and respect – everyone may be interviewing you!
9. Prepare for different types of interviews – one-on-one, sequential, serial, panel, group, behavioral, examination/text, and situational.
10. Be prepared to tactfully deal with illegal questions.
11. Know how to communicate both verbally and nonverbally.
12. Greet the interviewer properly – with a firm handshake and smile.
13. Wait to be to seated and avoid crossing your legs and arms.
14. Communicate positive behaviors during the first five minutes.
15. Let the interviewer initiate the openers.
16. Maintain good eye contact.
17. Answer questions with complete sentences and with substance.
18. Close the interview properly by summarizing your understanding, scheduling a second interview, or asking for the job.
19. Delay salary discussions until you've received a job offer.

Avoid Common Interview Errors

Unlike many other job search mistakes, interview errors tend to be **unforgiving**. This is the time when **first impressions** count the most. You need to **prepare well** and be on your **best behavior** – both verbal and nonverbal behaviors.

Employers have both positive and negative goals in mind. On the positive side, they want to hire someone who can do the job and add value or benefits to their organization. On the negative side, they are always looking for clues that tell them why they should **not** hire you. Make a mistake during the job interview and you may be instantly eliminated from further consideration. Therefore, you **must** be on your best behavior and avoid the many common mistakes interviewees make.

The following mistakes or errors are frequently cited by employers and job placement experts who have interviewed or worked with thousands of applicants:

1. Arrive late to the interview.
2. Makes a bad impression in the waiting area.
3. Offers poor and unacceptable excuses for behavior.
4. Presents an unattractive appearance and negative image.
5. Expresses bad, negative, and corrosive attitudes.
6. Engages in inappropriate and unexpected behaviors for an interview situation (shows tattoos, flirts, etc.).
7. Appears somewhat incoherent and unfocused.
8. Is inarticulate and uses poor grammar.
9. Gives short, incomplete, vague and uncertain answers.
10. Appears ill or has a possible undisclosed medical condition.

11. Volunteers personal information that normally would be illegal or inappropriate to ask.
12. Emits bad or irritating smells.
13. Shows little enthusiasm, drive, or initiative.
14. Lacks confidence and self-esteem.
15. Appears too eager and hungry for the job.
16. Communicates dishonesty or deception.
17. Demonstrates extreme role-playing to the point of being too smooth and superficial.
18. Appears evasive when asked about possible problems with background.
19. Speaks negatively of previous employers and co-workers.
20. Maintains poor eye contact.
21. Offers a limp or overly firm handshake.
22. Comes unprepared and shows little interest in the company.
23. Talks about salary and benefits early in the interview.
24. Is discourteous, ill-mannered, and disrespectful.
25. Appears socially awkward and/or odd.
26. Tells inappropriate jokes and laughs a lot.
27. Talks too much and too fast.
28. Argues with the interviewer.
29. Drops names to impress the interviewer.
30. Appears needy and greedy.
31. Fails to talk about accomplishments.
32. Does not ask questions about the job or employer.
33. Seems too effusive and self-effacing.
34. Appears self-centered rather than employer-centered.
35. Demonstrates poor listening skills.
36. Seems not bright enough for the job.
37. Doesn't know his/her worth and negotiate properly when it comes time to talk about compensation.
38. Closes the interview by just leaving.
39. Fails to schedule another interview and/or ask for the job.
40. Lacks appropriate follow-up skills, such as sending a thank-you note and making phone calls.

Handle Red Flags Tactfully

Most job seekers have one or more red flags in their background that could knock them out of consideration for a job. Some red flags appear on applications and resumes while others arise during interviews or background checks They include: lack of experience, under-educated, poor grades, criminal record, job hopping, poor references, over-qualified, bad credit, and fired. Be prepared to deal with your red flags in a positive manner – **admit the red flags but indicate what you have done to overcome them.** Always tell the truth, but do so in a positive manner that reflects on your ability to change your life for the better. For information on how to best respond to red flag questions, see *Job Interview Tips for People With Not-So-Hot Backgrounds* (Impact Publications, 2004) .

Red Flag #1: _____

Response: _____

_____

Red Flag #2: _____

Response: _____

_____

Red Flag #3: _____

Response: _____

_____

Prepare to Answer Key Questions

You need to develop positive answers to the most frequently asked interview questions. Perfect your answers with a mirror and tape recorder. Play back the tape and ask yourself:

- Do I show confidence and competence?
- Do I sound dynamic and enthusiastic?
- Do I talk in a conversational, non-memorized style?
- Do I speak without excessive fillers – *"ah," "like," "you know"*?
- Do I seem believable? Likable? Trustworthy?

Develop a **strategy** for your responses and the essence of the message you want to convey. **Do not memorize** responses. Be especially prepared to answer these three "killer" questions:

- **Tell me about yourself.** (Always focus on your work-related accomplishments – not your personal history)
- **Why should we hire you?** (Focus on your value/contributions)
- **What are your salary expectations?** (Timing is everything, and be careful what you wish for! See tips on page 52.)

The most **frequently asked questions** include the following:

Personality and Motivation

1. Why should we hire you?
2. Are you a self-starter?
3. What is your greatest strength? Weakness?
4. What would you most like to improve about yourself?
5. Describe your typical workday.
6. How well do you work under deadlines?
7. What will you bring to this position that others won't?
8. How well do you get along with your superiors? Co-workers?

9. Do you prefer working alone or with others?
10. How do others view your work?
11. How do you deal with criticism?
12. Do you consider yourself to be someone who takes greater initiative than others? Can you give an example?
13. Are you a good time manager?
14. How important is job security?
15. How do you define success?
16. How do you spend your leisure time?
17. What really motivates you to perform on the job?

Education and Training

18. Why didn't you go to college?
19. Why didn't you finish college?
20. Why did you major in _____?
21. Why weren't your grades better in school?
22. What subjects did you enjoy most? Least?
23. If you did it again, what would you change about your education?
24. What leadership positions did you hold in school?
25. What materials do you read regularly to keep up in your field?
26. What is the most recent skill you have learned?
27. What are your educational goals over the next few years?

Experience and Skills

28. Why do you want to leave your present job or previous jobs?
29. Why have you changed jobs so frequently?
30. What are your qualifications for this job?
31. What experiences prepared you for this job?
32. What did you like most about your present/most recent job?
33. What did you like least about that job?
34. What did you like most about your boss? Least?
35. Tell me which responsibilities you most enjoyed in your jobs.
36. What duties did you find most difficult to perform?
37. Why do you want to leave your present job? Being forced out?
38. Have you ever been fired or asked to resign?

39. What's the most important contribution you made on your job?
40. What did you want to accomplish but were unable to?
41. What's the most important thing you've learned from your jobs?

Career Goals

42. Tell me about yourself.
43. Describe your career goals.
44. How do your career goals today differ from five years ago?
45. Where do you see yourself five years from now?
46. Describe a major goal you set for yourself recently?
47. What are you doing to achieve that goal?
48. How long have you been looking for another job?

Why You Want This Job

49. Why do you want to work for us?
50. What do you see as your major contributions to our company?
51. What would you change about this position?
52. How long would you expect to stay with our company?
53. How do you feel about working overtime or on weekends?
54. Are you willing to relocate?
55. How much are you willing to travel?
56. What are your salary expectations?
57. How soon could you begin work?
58. Do you have any questions?

For more information, see these books (most on page 59):

- *Best Answers to 202 Job Interview Questions*
- *I Can't Believe They Asked Me That!*
- *Job Interview Tips for People With Not-So-Hot Backgrounds*
- *KeyWords to Nail Your Job Interview*
- *Nail the Job Interview!*
- *Win the Interview, Win the Job*
- *You Should Hire Me!*

Ask Informative Questions

You need to ask questions to elicit information **you** need about the position and organization; indeed, you want to know if the position is fit for you. In addition, the interviewer will be making judgments about you based on the questions you ask. You should ask questions concerning duties, responsibilities, training opportunities, advancement, and outlook. Avoid those dealing with salary and benefits. Also, avoid becoming an interrogator by asking too many questions – four to five key questions may be just right. Try a few of these for starters:

- What duties and responsibilities does the job entail?
- Where does this position fit into the organization?
- Is this a new position?
- What are you looking for in a successful candidate?
- When was the last person promoted?
- Is this position vacant now? Why? For how long?
- What is the best experience and background for this position?
- What expectations do you have for this position long-term?
- Whom would I report to? Tell me a little about these people. What are their strengths and weaknesses?
- What is the most difficult challenge facing this position?
- What problems might I expect to encounter on this job?
- What has been done recently in regards to . . . .?
- Tell me about promotions and advancement with this company.
- What are your expectations for the person hired for this job?
- Where do you see this company five years from now? Ten?

Having prepared a written list of questions, many interviewees wonder if it's okay to write them down and take them to the interview. Do so since it also indicates you are interested.

Close & Exit the Interview Properly

It is important to close the job interview with **understanding, enthusiasm, and desire**. Revealing your **spark** can make a difference between being rejected or accepted for the job. Interviewers normally initiate the close by standing, shaking hands, and thanking you for coming to the interview. They may express some variation of *"Glad you could come by today. We have several other candidates to interview. We'll be in touch."* In response, most interviewees shake hands, thank the interviewer, leave, and hope for the best. Don't do this! Such a closing and exit almost ensures that you will not be called back for another interview or offered the job. It's critical that you use this time to close and exit the interview to your advantage.

Indeed, **hope and waiting** are not good job search strategies! At this stage, you should **summarize the interview** in terms of your interests, strengths, and goals. Briefly restate your qualifications and interest in working with the employer. For example, an accountant might summarize as follows:

> *I'm really glad I had the chance to talk with you. I know, with what I learned when I reorganized the accounting department at XYZ Corporation, I could increase your profits, too.*

If you really want the job, close by asking for another interview or the job. **Show desire** by telling the interviewer you want to work for them. For example, you might close saying:

> *Even though I'm looking at other opportunities, this is really the place I would love to work. It's where I know I can make a difference. Can we schedule another interview within the next week?*

Follow Up the Interview Quickly

Follow-up is the key to unlocking employers' doors and for achieving job search success. But many people fear following up – think they are bothering the employer or have nothing more to say. Unfortunately, they would rather wait to hear from the employer than to take actions that could influence the final hiring decision. Here's a simple truth: **waiting** is not a good job search strategy for getting a job offer!

Without an effective follow-up campaign, you may be passed over for the job. If you want interviewers to know that you are interested in their position, you need to follow up with a nice **thank-you letter** and/or **phone call**, in which you restate your strongest talents. At this stage, **timing is everything**.

Shortly after the interview – later the same day – send a nice **thank-you letter** by email and mail. In this letter:

1. Express your appreciation for the interviewer's time.
2. Indicate your continued interest in the position.
3. Restate any special skills or experience you would bring to the job (keep this brief and well focused).
4. Close by mentioning that you will call in a few days to inquire about the employer's decision.

A **telephone call** will remind the employer of your continued interest and enthusiasm for the position. It gives you a chance to have a final interview by phone. For examples of follow-up letters, see *Nail the Cover Letter!* and *201 Dynamite Job Search Letters* (Impact Publications) on page 59.

Avoid 20 Salary Mistakes

Job seekers make several **salary negotiation errors**, which often result in knocking them out of further consideration or they receive a lower salary than what they could have gotten had they followed a few salary tips. Several of these errors also may leave a bad impression – you have a poor attitude, you're "difficult," or you're basically a self-centered job seeker who primarily focuses on salary and benefits rather than on the performance needs of the employer and organization. The most frequent errors you should **avoid** include:

1. Wishful thinking – believe you're worth more than you are worth.
2. Appear to be a clever and manipulative person playing games.
3. Neglect to research salary options and comparables.
4. Fail to communicate accomplishments when talking about money.
5. Reveal salary expectations on the resume or in a letter.
6. Answer the question *"What are your salary requirements?"* before being offered the job.
7. Raise the salary question before the employer does.
8. Fail to ask "value" questions about the company and job.
9. Ask *"Is this offer negotiable?"*
10. Quickly accept the first offer without considering options.
11. Accept the offer on the spot.
12. Agree to the offer primarily because of compensation.
13. Try to negotiate compensation during the first interview.
14. Forget to consider benefits and thus only focus on salary.
15. Negotiate a salary figure rather than discuss a salary range.
16. Haggle over the telephone or by email.
17. Focus on your needs rather than the employer's needs.
18. Try to play "hardball" by engaging in tough negotiations and mentioning alternative offers, which may or may not be true.
19. Express a negative attitude toward the employer's offer.
20. Talk too much and listen too little.

Accept the Job Offer

It's okay to take notes when negotiating salary. Be sure to jot down pertinent information about the terms of employment. At the end of the session, before you get up to leave, **summarize** what you understand will be included in the compensation package and show it in outline form to the employer. Make sure you and the employer **understand the terms of employment**, especially the compensation package.

If you accept the position, ask the employer to **put the offer in writing**, which may be in the form of a **letter of agreement**. This document should spell out your duties and responsibilities as well as detail how you will be compensated. If your agreement includes incentivized pay, make sure it details exactly how your commissions or bonuses will work – how and when they will be paid, set up, and measured. For example, will you be paid at the end of each quarter or at the end of year? Do you receive a flat bonus, such as $1,000, or a percentage of the sales from an income stream?

Ask the employer to **email or fax you a copy** of this document for your review. Let him know you'll get back with him immediately. This document will serve as your **employment contract**.

You should do two other things before showing up for work:

1. Send your new employer a nice thank-you letter – **never underestimate the power of a thank-you letter.**
2. Send thank-you letters to those who assisted you with all phases of your job search.

Survive and Thrive on the Job

How can you best ensure keeping your job as well as advancing your career in the future? How can you best avoid becoming a victim of cutbacks, politics, and terminations?

Most employers want their employees to perform according to certain **expectations**. Above all else, they want **truthfulness, honesty, and value** from employees. They expect workers to:

1. Be on time consistently.
2. Follow directions.
3. Be dependable in everything they do.
4. Get the job done quickly, starting with things they least like to do.
5. Do the job well and with a positive attitude.
6. Take initiative rather than wait to be given directions.
7. Be accurate and show competence.
8. Dress and groom appropriately – conservative and professional.
9. Maintain good health and cleanliness.
10. Be enthusiastic and energetic.
11. Be a loyal employee who looks out for the company and boss.
12. Avoid doing personal business on company time.
13. Solve problems skillfully.
14. Be pleasant to work with and to be around.
15. Avoid conflicts and arguments with others.
16. Help out when needed, even if doing so is not part of the job.
17. Be unselfish and give credit to others, especially the boss.
18. Persevere in spite of unusual challenges and difficulties.
19. Take responsibility for their job and everything they do.
20. Make useful suggestions and find creative ways to solve problems.
21. Earn the respect of fellow workers.
22. Become a good team player.
23. Be savvy in managing any office politics.

10 Job Survival Strategies

The following 10 survival strategies can be used to minimize the uncertainty and instability surrounding many jobs today:

1. Learn to read the signs of coming changes.
2. Document your achievements.
3. Toot your horn for promotion.
4. Expand your horizons by learning new skills.
5. Prepare for your next job by acquiring more job experience, education, and training.
6. Find and work with a good mentor.
7. Continue networking both on and off the job.
8. Use your Motivated Abilities and Skills (MAS).
9. Think and behave like an entrepreneur.
10. Keep a positive attitude even when times get tough.

Conduct an Annual Career Check-Up

To keep your career healthy, you should conduct an annual career check-up. At least once a year you should take out your resume and review it. Ask yourself these questions:

- Am I achieving my goals and purpose in life?
- Has my objective changed? If "yes," what is it now?
- Is this job meeting my expectations? If "no," why not?
- Am I doing what I'm good at and enjoy doing?
- Are my skills up-to-date for this job and organization?
- Am I fully using my skills as well as acquiring new skills?
- Does this company fully value my contributions?
- Is this job worth keeping or should I "test the water"?
- How can I best achieve career satisfaction?
- What other opportunities might be better than this job?

Personal Information

Provide basic personal information that might appear on a job application or resume, including a street mailing address.

Name (full) _____

Street address _____

_____

City _____

State _____

Zip Code _____

Other mailing address _____

_____

Home phone _____

Cell phone _____

Fax number _____

Pager number _____

Email address _____

Date of birth _____

Place of birth _____

Social Security # ___(memorize or secure elsewhere)___

Driver's license # _____

Key Contacts/Directory

Name _____

Address _____

Phone _____ Email _____

Name _____

Address _____

Phone _____ Email _____

Name _____

Address _____

Phone _____ Email _____

Name _____

Address _____

Phone _____ Email _____

Name _____

Address _____

Phone _____ Email _____

Name _____

Address _____

Phone _____ Email _____

Order Form/Resources

These resources are available from Impact Publications. Full descriptions of each can be found at www.impactpublications.com. Complete this form or list titles, include shipping ($5 plus 9% of the subtotal), enclose payment, and send your order to:

IMPACT PUBLICATIONS
9104-N Manassas Drive
Manassas Park, VA 20111-5211
Tel. 1-800-361-1055, 703-361-7300 or Fax 703-335-9486
Online ordering: www.impactpublications.com

Qty.	Titles	Price	TOTAL
Military Spouses			
___	The 2-Second Commute	$14.99	___
___	Armed Forces Guide to Personal Financial Planning	22.95	___
___	Chicken Soup for the Military Wife's Soul	14.95	___
___	The Complete Idiot's Guide to Life as a Military Spouse	12.95	___
___	A Family's Guide to the Military for Dummies	19.99	___
___	Help! I'm a Military Spouse – I Get a Life Too!	15.99	___
___	Heroes At Home	13.99	___
___	Homefront Club	19.95	___
___	In Harm's Way	16.00	___
___	Jobs and the Military Spouse	17.95	___
___	New Relocating Spouse's Guide to Employment	32.95	___
___	Married to the Military	14.00	___
___	Military Spouse Finance Guide	19.95	___
___	Military Spouse's Complete Guide to Career Success	17.95	___
___	Navy Spouse's Guide	21.95	___
___	Surviving Deployment	19.95	___
___	Today's Military Wife	19.95	___
___	Virtual Assistant	29.95	___
___	Your Military Family Network	24.95	___

Career Transition for Military Personnel
___ Marketing Yourself for a Second Career DVD 79.95 _____
___ Military-to-Civilian Resumes and Letters 21.95 _____
___ Military Transition to Civilian Success 21.95 _____

Military Pocket Guides (bulk discounts on page 60)
___ Military Personal Finance Pocket Guide 2.95 _____
___ Military Spouse's Employment Pocket Guide 2.95 _____
___ Military Spouse's Map Through the Maze 2.95 _____
___ Military-to-Civilian Transition Pocket Guide 2.95 _____

Job Interviews and Salary Negotiations
___ Best Answers to 202 Job Interview Questions 17.95 _____
___ Give Me More Money! 17.95 _____
___ I Can't Believe They Asked Me That! 17.95 _____
___ Nail the Job Interview! 14.95 _____
___ Win the Interview, Win the Job 15.95 _____

Resumes and Letters
___ 201 Dynamite Job Search Letters 19.95 _____
___ High Impact Resumes and Letters 19.95 _____
___ Nail the Cover Letter! 17.95 _____

Attitude, Motivation, Goals, Skills
___ 100 Ways to Motivate Yourself 14.99 _____
___ Attitude Is Everything 14.95 _____
___ Goals! 16.95 _____
___ I Want to Do Something Else,
    But I'm Not Sure What It Is 15.95 _____
___ Success Principles 16.95 _____

Federal Government Jobs (see page 16)
___ The Book of U.S. Government Jobs 22.95 _____
___ Federal Resume Guidebook 21.95 _____
___ Ten Steps to a Federal Job, With CD-ROM 28.95 _____

_____

SUBTOTAL _____
Shipping ($5 + 9% of SUBTOTAL) _____
TOTAL ORDER ------------------------------- _____

Military Spouses and Transition Pocket Guides

Cost-effective resources from 59¢ to $2.95 each!

- Military Spouse's Employment Pocket Guide
- Military Spouse's Map Through the Maze Pocket Guide
- Military-to-Civilian Transition Pocket Guide
- Military Personal Finance Pocket Guide

Quantity discounts:

1 copy	$2.95	500 copies	$663.75
10 copies	$23.60	1,000 copies	$1,180.00
25 copies	$51.63	5,000 copies	$5,162.50
50 copies	$88.50	25,000 copies	$22,125.00
100 copies	$147.50	50,00 copies	$36,875.00
		100,000 copies	$59,000.00

ORDERS AND QUANTITY DISCOUNTS:
1-800-361-1055 or www.impactpublications.com